P9-EJI-401

THE WISDOM OF THE PSALMS

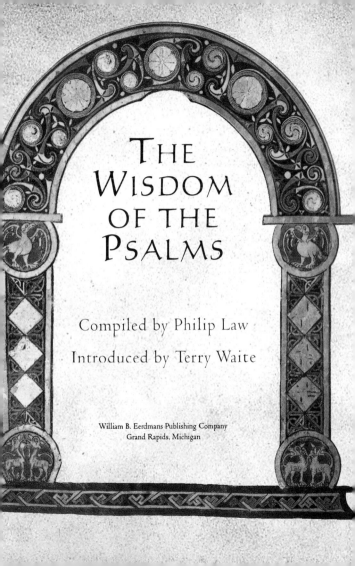

THE
WISDOM
OF THE
PSALMS

Compiled by Philip Law

Introduced by Terry Waite

William B. Eerdmans Publishing Company
Grand Rapids, Michigan

Copyright © 1996 Lion Publishing

This edition published 1996 in the USA
through special arrangement with
Lion Publishing by
Wm. B. Eerdmans Publishing Co.
255 Jefferson Ave. S.E., Grand Rapids,
Michigan 49503

All rights reserved

Printed in Singapore

01 00 99 98 97 96   7 6 5 4 3 2 1

ISBN 0-8028-3831-6

Contents

Introduction   6

Adoration   11

Meditation   19

Confession   27

Suffering and Hope   35

Blessing and Joy   41

INTRODUCTION

Throughout the ages the psalms have been recognized as a source of spiritual wisdom and also as great poetry. It has been the practice of the Greek and Roman Churches to recite all of the psalms weekly. The Anglican Church, taking a slightly more relaxed pace, settled for a monthly recitation. There have been certain individuals for whom the psalms figured so prominently in their private devotions that it is said they recited all one hundred and fifty psalms each day.

In the early church the psalms were so well known by working people that they used to sing them when they were at work in the fields or the home. Then they enjoyed the status that a pop song might have today.

Whilst the psalms have a central place in Christian worship and prayer they have their roots in Jewish spirituality. These ancient verses were used long before the coming of Christ and therefore in Christian usage the original thoughts of the writers are transformed in the light of Christianity.

Many of the psalms speak on behalf of a small group of people who feel rejected and downtrodden. The writers encourage the weak and urge them to remain faithful to the commands of God. The psalms were also used to sing the praises of God.

It has been said that they embody the literary genius of the Hebrew nation. Certainly their rhythmic harmony and beauty have stood the test of time.

The psalms as originally written do present the modern reader with certain difficulties in regard to their expressed attitude towards the enemies of Israel. The strong words of the psalms can only be understood if we step back and attempt to see life through the eyes of their authors. They were passionately concerned with keeping the people faithful to God and his commands. The concerns of God were identified with those of his faithful people, so that any insult to any of them was seen as an insult to God himself.

When God, who is all-holy, is in contact with sin, then a reaction occurs and punishment must follow. We are all familiar with the ancient Hebrew saying 'an eye for an eye, and a tooth for a tooth'.

The revelation of the nature and love of God as seen in the death and resurrection of Christ transformed the church's understanding of the psalms, including the difficult passages. In reading the psalms we need to keep in mind that in understanding them and using them in our own prayers we may interpret them in the light of the Christian revelation.

It is of great interest to note how individual verses of the psalms have been used to confirm or support a point of view or to give guidance for a life. By understanding how the psalms have been used we can gain an insight into history and into the thought patterns of those who used them. There is only space in this brief introduction to cite a few examples.

In 1750 the Bishop of Oxford and later Archbishop of Canterbury preached the 'earthquake' sermon on Psalm 2:11. A serious earthquake in March 1750 caused thousands to camp outdoors and by preaching on this text the good bishop was able to calm serious panic.

Psalm 3 was one of the psalms designated to be used following the defeat of the Spanish Armada (1588). At the time the full extent of the victory was not known and England was somewhat nervous in regard to her enemies.

Finally, Psalm 92:7. In the sixteenth century a classical scholar by the name of Isaac Casaubon was gently sailing on the river Seine. Unfortunately his boat was struck by a barge and he lost his psalter which he had used for some twenty-two years. At the time of this unfortunate accident both he and his wife were singing Psalm 92 and had reached verse 7. Isaac wrote: 'I could not but remember that place of St Ambrose where he says that this is the peculiarity of the Book of Psalms, that every one can use its words as if they were peculiarly and individually his own.'

Perhaps St Ambrose should have the final word, for he is undoubtedly right. The psalms are unique. They have a long and fascinating history and across the years have been understood in a variety of ways. This book makes the psalms available to those who would wish to use them in the spirit of St Ambrose. The children of Israel have given us a priceless treasure. Let us use and enjoy it.

TERRY WAITE

March 1996

ADORATION

I

Give thanks to the Lord of lords...
In wisdom he made the heavens.

From Psalm 136

GOD'S GREATNESS

O Lord, our Lord,
your greatness is seen in all the world!
Your praise reaches up to the heavens;
it is sung by children and babies.
You are safe and secure from all your enemies;
you stop anyone who opposes you.
When I look at the sky, which you have made,
at the moon and the stars,
which you set in their places—
what are human beings, that you think of them;
mere mortals, that you care for them?
Yet you made them inferior only to yourself;
you crowned them with glory and honour.
You appointed them rulers
over everything you made;
you placed them over all creation:
sheep and cattle, and the wild animals too;
the birds and the fish and the creatures in the seas.
O Lord, our Lord,
your greatness is seen in all the world!

Psalm 8

SILENT WITNESSES

The heavens are telling the glory of God;
and the firmament proclaims his handiwork.
Day to day pours forth speech,
and night to night declares knowledge.
There is no speech, nor are there words;
their voice is not heard;
yet their voice goes out through all the earth,
and their words to the end of the world.

From Psalm 19

GOD EVERYWHERE

O Lord, thou hast searched me, and known me.
Thou knowest my downsitting and mine uprising,
  thou understandest my thought afar off.
Thou compassest my path and my lying down,
and art acquainted with all my ways.
For there is not a word in my tongue,
but, lo, O Lord, thou knowest it altogether.
Thou hast beset me behind and before,
  and laid thine hand upon me.
Such knowledge is too wonderful for me;
  it is high, I cannot attain unto it.
Whither shall I go from thy spirit?
or whither shall I flee from thy presence?
If I ascend up into heaven, thou art there:
if I make my bed in hell, behold, thou art there.
If I take the wings of the morning,
and dwell in the uttermost parts of the sea;
Even there shall thy hand lead me,
and thy right hand shall hold me.

If I say, Surely the darkness shall cover me;
even the night shall be light about me.
Yea, the darkness hideth not from thee;
but the night shineth as the day:
the darkness and the light are both alike to thee...
Search me, O God, and know my heart:
try me, and know my thoughts:
And see if there be any wicked way in me,
and lead me in the way everlasting.

From Psalm 139

GOD'S CREATION

Bless the Lord, O my soul.
O Lord my God, thou art very great;
thou art clothed with honour and majesty.
Who coverest thyself with light as with a garment:
who stretchest out the heavens like a curtain:
Who layeth the beams of his chambers in the waters:
who maketh the clouds his chariot:
who walketh upon the wings of the wind:
Who maketh his angels spirits;
his ministers a flaming fire:
Who laid the foundations of the earth,
that it should not be removed for ever.
Thou coveredst it with the deep as with a garment:
the waters stood above the mountains.
At thy rebuke they fled;
at the voice of thy thunder they hasted away...

Thou makest darkness, and it is night:
wherein all the beasts of the forest do creep forth.
The young lions roar after their prey,
and seek their meat from God.
The sun ariseth, they gather themselves together,
and lay them down in their dens.
Man goeth forth unto his work
and to his labour until the evening.
O Lord, how manifold are thy works!
in wisdom hast thou made them all:
the earth is full of thy riches...
Thou hidest thy face, they are troubled:
thou takest away their breath, they die,
and return to their dust.
Thou sendest forth thy spirit, they are created:
and thou renewest the face of the earth.

From Psalm 104

GOD'S TENDER POWER

Great is Yahweh and worthy of all praise,
his greatness beyond all reckoning.
Each age will praise your deeds to the next,
proclaiming your mighty works...
They will speak of your awesome power,
and I shall recount your greatness...
Yahweh is tenderness and pity,
slow to anger, full of faithful love.
Yahweh is generous to all,
his tenderness embraces all his creatures.
All your creatures shall thank you, Yahweh,
and your faithful shall bless you...
Yahweh is trustworthy in all his words,
and upright in all his deeds.
Yahweh supports all who stumble,
lifts up those who are bowed down...
Upright in all that he does,
Yahweh acts only in faithful love.
He is close to all who call upon him,
all who call on him from the heart.

From Psalm 145

MEDITATION

7

Be still, and know that I am God.

From Psalm 46

SPIRITUAL GROWTH

Blessed is the man
who does not walk in the counsel
of the wicked
or stand in the way of sinners
or sit in the seat of mockers.
But his delight is in the law of the Lord,
and on his law he meditates day and night.
He is like a tree planted by streams of water,
which yields its fruit in season
and whose leaf does not wither.
Whatever he does prospers.
Not so the wicked!
They are like chaff that the wind blows away.
Therefore the wicked will not stand
in the judgment,
nor sinners in the assembly of the righteous.
For the Lord watches over the way
of the righteous,
but the way of the wicked will perish.

Psalm 1

PERFECT WISDOM

The law of the Lord is perfect,
reviving the soul;
the decrees of the Lord are sure,
making wise the simple;
the precepts of the Lord are right,
rejoicing the heart;
the commandment of the Lord is clear,
enlightening the eyes;
the fear of the Lord is pure,
enduring forever.

From Psalm 19

THE USELESSNESS OF RICHES

My mouth shall speak of wisdom;
and the meditation of my heart shall be of understanding.
I will incline mine ear to a parable:
I will open my dark saying upon the harp...
They that trust in their wealth,
and boast themselves in the multitude of their riches;
None of them can by any means redeem his brother,
nor give to God a ransom for him...
That he should still live for ever, and not see corruption.
For he seeth that wise men die,
likewise the fool and the brutish person perish,
and leave their wealth to others.
Their inward thought is,
that their houses shall continue for ever,
and their dwelling places to all generations;
they call their lands after their own names.

Nevertheless man being in honour abideth not:
he is like the beasts that perish.
This their way is their folly:
yet their posterity approve their sayings.
Like sheep they are laid in the grave;
death shall feed on them;
and the upright shall have dominion over them
in the morning;
and their beauty shall consume in the grave
from their dwelling,...
Man that is in honour, and understandeth not,
is like the beasts that perish.

From Psalm 49

The Beginning of Wisdom

Great are the works of the Lord,
pondered over by all who delight in them.
His deeds are full of majesty and splendour...
the Lord is gracious and compassionate...
His works are truth and justice;
all his precepts are trustworthy,
established to endure for ever,
enacted in faithfulness and truth...
The fear of the Lord is the beginning of wisdom,
and they who live by it grow in understanding.

From Psalm 111

TEACH ME YOUR WAYS

How sweet are your words to my taste,
sweeter than honey to my mouth!
I gain understanding from your precepts;
therefore I hate every wrong path.
Your word is a lamp to my feet
and a light for my path.
I have taken an oath and confirmed it,
that I will follow your righteous laws.
I have suffered much;
renew my life, O Lord, according to your word.
Accept, O Lord, the willing praise of my mouth,
and teach me your laws...
Your statutes are my heritage for ever;
they are the joy of my heart.
My heart is set on keeping your decrees
to the very end.

From Psalm 119

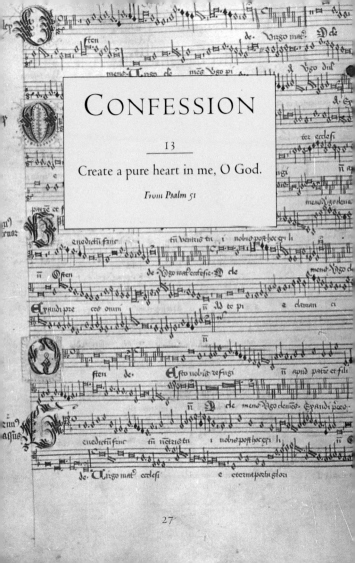

CONFESSION

13

Create a pure heart in me, O God.

From Psalm 51

27

God's Unfailing Love

Make your paths known to me, Lord;
teach me your ways.
Lead me by your faithfulness and teach me,
for you are God my saviour;
in you I put my hope all day long.
Remember, Lord, your tender care and love unfailing,
for they are from of old.
Do not remember the sins and offences of my youth,
but remember me in your unfailing love.
The Lord is good and upright;
therefore he teaches sinners the way they should go.
He guides the humble in right conduct,
and teaches them his way...
My eyes are ever on the Lord,
who alone can free my feet from the net.
Turn to me and show me your favour,
for I am lonely and oppressed.
Relieve the troubles of my heart
and lead me out of my distress.
Look on my affliction and misery
and forgive me every sin.

From Psalm 25

PURIFY MY HEART

Have mercy on me, O God, in your faithful love,
in your great tenderness wipe away my offences;
wash me clean from my guilt,
purify me from my sin.
For I am well aware of my offences,
my sin is constantly in mind.
Against you, you alone, I have sinned.
I have done what you see to be wrong,
that you may show your saving justice
when you pass sentence,
and your victory may appear
when you give judgement.
Remember, I was born guilty,
a sinner from the moment of conception.
But you delight in sincerity of heart,
and in secret you teach me wisdom.

From Psalm 51

Teach Us to Number our Days

Lord, thou hast been our dwelling place in all generations.
Before the mountains were brought forth,
or ever thou hadst formed the earth and the world,
even from everlasting to everlasting, thou art God.
Thou turnest man to destruction;
and sayest, Return, ye children of men.
For a thousand years in thy sight
are but as yesterday when it is past,
and as a watch in the night.

Thou carriest them away as with a flood;
they are as a sleep:
in the morning they are like grass which groweth up.
In the morning it flourisheth, and groweth up;
in the evening it is cut down, and withereth.
For we are consumed by thine anger,
and by thy wrath are we troubled.
Thou hast set our iniquities before thee,
our secret sins in the light of thy countenance.

For all our days are passed away in thy wrath:
we spend our years as a tale that is told.
The days of our years are threescore years and ten;
and if by reason of strength they be fourscore years,
yet is their strength labour and sorrow;
for it is soon cut off, and we fly away.
Who knoweth the power of thine anger?
even according to thy fear, so is thy wrath.
So teach us to number our days,
that we may apply our hearts unto wisdom.

From Psalm 90

My Heart's Desire

My feet had almost slipped,
my foothold had all but given way,
because boasters roused my envy
when I saw how the wicked prosper.
No painful suffering for them!
They are sleek and sound in body;
Therefore they wear pride like a necklace
and violence like a robe that wraps them round...
I set my mind to understand this
but I found it too hard for me,
until I went into God's sanctuary,
where I saw clearly what their destiny would be...
My mind was embittered,
and I was pierced to the heart.
I was too brutish to understand,
in your sight, God, no better than a beast.
Yet I am always with you;
you hold my right hand.
You guide me by your counsel
and afterwards you will receive me with glory.

Whom have I in
heaven but you?
And having you,
I desire nothing else
on earth.
Though heart and
body fail,
yet God is the rock
of my heart,
my portion for ever.

From Psalm 73

A CRY FOR HELP

From the depths of my despair
I call to you, Lord.
Hear my cry, O Lord;
listen to my call for help!
If you kept a record of our sins,
who could escape being condemned?
But you forgive us,
so that we should stand in awe of you.
I wait eagerly for the Lord's help,
and in his word I trust.

From Psalm 130

SUFFERING
AND HOPE

19

Cast thy burden on the Lord,
and he shall sustain thee.

From Psalm 55

TERROR NO MORE

Why are you so far away, O Lord?
Why do you hide yourself when we are in trouble?
The wicked are proud and persecute the poor...
the greedy curse and reject the Lord...
They lie in wait for the poor;
they catch them in their traps and drag them away.
The helpless victims lie crushed;
brute strength has defeated them.
The wicked say to themselves, 'God doesn't care!
He has closed his eyes and will never see me!'...
But you do see;
you take notice of trouble and suffering
and are always ready to help...
You will listen, O Lord, to the prayers of the lowly;
you will give them courage.
You will hear the cries of the oppressed
and the orphans;
you will judge in their favour,
so that mortal men may cause terror no more.

From Psalm 10

WHERE IS GOD?

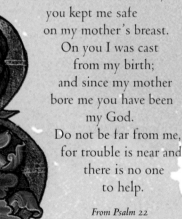

My God, my God, why have you forsaken me?
Why are you so far from helping me,
from the words of my groaning?
O my God, I cry by day, but you do not answer,
and by night, but find no rest...
Yet it was you who took me from the womb;
you kept me safe
on my mother's breast.
On you I was cast
from my birth;
and since my mother
bore me you have been
my God.
Do not be far from me,
for trouble is near and
there is no one
to help.

From Psalm 22

NEAR TO THE BROKEN-HEARTED

Who among you delights in life,
longs for time to enjoy prosperity?
Guard your tongue from evil,
your lips from any breath of deceit.
Turn away from evil and do good,
seek peace and pursue it.
The eyes of Yahweh are on the upright,
his ear turned to their cry.
But Yahweh's face is set against those who do evil,
to cut off the memory of them from the earth.
They cry in anguish and Yahweh hears,
and rescues them from all their troubles.
Yahweh is near to the broken-hearted,
he helps those whose spirit is crushed.

From Psalm 34

HOPE IN GOD

Show me, O Lord, my life's end
and the number of my days;
let me know how fleeting is my life.
You have made my days a mere handbreadth;
the span of my years is as nothing before you.
Each man's life is but a breath.
Man is a mere phantom as he goes to and fro:
He bustles about, but only in vain;
he heaps up wealth,
not knowing who will get it.
But now, Lord, what do I look for?
My hope is in you...
listen to my cry for help;
be not deaf to my weeping.
For I dwell with you as an alien,
a stranger, as all my fathers were.
Look away from me,
that I may rejoice again
before I depart and am no more.

From Psalm 39

LONGING FOR GOD

As a deer longs for flowing streams,
so my soul longs for you, O God.
My soul thirsts for God,
for the living God.
When shall I come and behold the face of God?

From Psalm 42

BLESSING
AND JOY

25

You will show me the path
that leads to life;
your presence fills me with joy
for ever.

From Psalm 16

God My Shepherd

The Lord is my shepherd;
I shall not want.
He maketh me to lie down in green pastures:
he leadeth me beside the still waters.
He restoreth my soul:
he leadeth me in the paths of righteousness
for his name's sake.
Yea, though I walk through the valley of
the shadow of death,
I will fear no evil:
for thou art with me;
thy rod and thy staff they comfort me.
Thou preparest a table before me
in the presence of mine enemies:
thou anointest my head with oil;
my cup runneth over.
Surely goodness and mercy shall follow me
all the days of my life:
and I will dwell in the house of the Lord for ever.

Psalm 23

LASTING JOY

O Lord my God, I cried unto thee,
and thou hast healed me.
O Lord, thou hast brought up my soul from the grave:
thou hast kept me alive,
that I should not go down to the pit.
Sing unto the Lord...
and give thanks at the remembrance of his holiness.
For his anger endureth but a moment;
in his favour is life:
weeping may endure for a night,
but joy cometh in the morning.

From Psalm 30

TRUST IN THE LORD

Do not be vexed because of evildoers
or envy those who do wrong.
For like the grass they soon wither,
and like green pasture they fade away.
Trust in the Lord and do good...
Delight in the Lord,
and he will grant you your heart's desire.
Commit your way to the Lord;
trust in him, and he will act.
He will make your righteousness shine clear as the day
and the justice of your cause like the brightness of noon.

From Psalm 37

Better than Life

God, you are my God,
I pine for you;
my heart thirsts for you,
my body longs for you,
as a land parched, dreary and waterless.
Thus I have gazed on you in the sanctuary,
seeing your power and your glory.
Better your faithful love than life itself;
my lips will praise you...
For you have always been my help;
in the shadow of your wings I rejoice.

From Psalm 63

GOD'S ENDURING MERCY

The Lord is merciful and gracious,
slow to anger, and plenteous in mercy.
He will not always chide:
neither will he keep his anger for ever.
He hath not dealt with us after our sins;
nor rewarded us according to our iniquities.
For as the heaven is high above the earth,
so great is his mercy toward them that fear him.
As far as the east is from the west,
so far hath he removed our transgressions from us.

Like as a father pitieth his children,
so the Lord pitieth them that fear him.
For he knoweth our frame;
he remembereth that we are dust.
As for man, his days are as grass:
as a flower of the field, so he flourisheth.
For the wind passeth over it, and it is gone;
and the place thereof shall know it no more.
But the mercy of the Lord
is from everlasting to everlasting
upon them that fear him,
and his righteousness unto children's children;

From Psalm 103

ACKNOWLEDGMENTS

Text Acknowledgments

Extracts from the Authorised Version of the Bible (The King James Bible), the rights of which are vested in the Crown, are reproduced by permission of the Crown's Patentee, Cambridge University Press: pages 14-15, 16-17, 19, 22-23, 30-31, 35, 42, 43, 46-47.Scriptures quoted from the *Good News Bible* published by The Bible Societies/HarperCollins Publishers Ltd UK © American Bible Society, 1966, 1971, 1976, 1992: pages 12, 27, 34, 36, 41.Scripture quotations taken from the HOLY BIBLE, NEW INTERNATIONAL VERSION. Copyright © 1973, 1978, 1984 by International Bible Society. Used by permission of Hodder & Stoughton Ltd. All rights reserved: pages 20, 25, 39.New Jerusalem Bible © 1985 by Darton, Longman and Todd Ltd and Doubleda and Company, Inc.: pages 11, 18, 29, 38, 45.Scripture text marked NRSV is from the New Revised Standard Version of the Bible, copyright © 1989 by the Division of Christian Education of the National Council of the Churches of Christ in the USA: pages 13, 21, 37, 40. Revised English Bible © 1989 by permission of Oxford and Cambridge University Presses: pages 24, 28, 33, 44.

Picture Acknowledgments

1: The Bodleian Library, Oxford, MS Douce 131, fol. 68v; 2/3 and cover: BL 9313 Cott Vesp A | f.30v King David with his court musicians, English (Canterbury), c.730 Vespasian Psalter (c.730 British Library, London/Bridgeman Art Library, London; 4: The Bodleian Library, Oxford, MS Hatton 1, fol. 3.2; 7: The Bodleian Library, Oxford, MS. Hatton 1, fol. 3.4; 8: LAM59017 Ms 233 f.145v Historiated Initial 'C' (Cantate Domino) with three clerics singing and a musician playing the viol, English, Vaux Psalter (early 14th century) Lambeth Palace Library, London/Bridgeman Art Library, London; 11 and cover: The Bodleian Library, Oxford, reproduced by permission of the Provost and Fellows of Eton College; 13: The Bodleian Library, Oxford, MS Douce 293, fol. 54b; 15: The Bodleian Library, Oxford, MS. Douce 293, fol. 16r; 17: BL 67792 Har | 4940 f.28 Astronomical Theological diagram with angels turning the world, from the Breviari D'Amor, British Library, London/Bridgeman Art Library, London; 19: The Bodleian Library, Oxford, reproduced by permission of the Provost and Fellows of Eton College; 20/21: The Bodleian Library, Oxford, MS. Douce 202, fol. 2r; 23: The Bodleian Library, Oxford, MS Douce 293, fol.103r; 24: The Bodleian Library, Oxford, University College MS. 100, fol. 18v, reproduced by permission of the Master and Fellows of University College, Oxford; 27: The Bodleian Library, Oxford, reproduced by permission of the Provost and Fellows of Eton College; 30: The Bodleian Library, Oxford, MS. Douce 293, fol. 78r; 33: The Bodleian Library, Oxford, MS. Douce 293, fol. 2r; 35: The Bodleian Library, Oxford, reproduced by permission of the Provost and Fellows of Eton College; 37: The Bodleian Library, Oxford, MS Douce 293, fol. 121v; 41: The Bodleian Library, Oxford, reproduced by permission of the Provost and Fellows of Eton College; 43: The Bodleian Library, Oxford, MS. Douce 293, fol. 29r; 46: The Bodleian Library, Oxford, MS Douce 293, fol. 115r.

Artwork

Amanda Barlow, Jane Thomson and Vanessa Card